Oxford Levels Placement and Progress Kit

CW00460374

Workbook 7

This book belongs to:

_____

Activities by Jane Wood
Series created by Roderick Hunt and Alex Brychta

OXFORD
UNIVERSITY PRESS

OXFORD
UNIVERSITY PRESS

Great Clarendon Street, Oxford, OX2 6DP, United Kingdom

Oxford University Press is a department of the University of Oxford. It furthers the University's objective of excellence in research, scholarship, and education by publishing worldwide. Oxford is a registered trade mark of Oxford University Press in the UK and in certain other countries.

First published 2019

British Library Cataloguing in Publication Data

Data available

ISBN: 978-0-1984-4528-9

10 9 8 7 6 5 4 3 2 1

Paper used in the production of this book is a natural, recyclable product made from wood grown in sustainable forests. The manufacturing process conforms to the environmental regulations of the country of origin.

Printed in China by Golden Cup Printing Co Ltd

Acknowledgements

Series consultant: Catherine Baker

Activities by: Jane Wood

The publisher would like to thank the following for permission to reproduce photographs: **p37(m)**: Visuals Unlimited, Inc./Art Morris; **p37(b)**: Reinhard Dirscherl/Science Photo Library; **p45(b)**: NOAA/SCIENCE PHOTO LIBRARY; **p46(t)**: YOSHIKAZU TSUNO/AFP/Getty Images; **p46(b)**: jmsilva/Getty Images; **p47(t)**: Photography by Fred Zhang/Getty Images; **p47(b)**: georgeclerk/iStockphoto; **p54(t)**: dave stamboulis/Alamy Stock Photo; **p55(b)**: Andrew Haliburton/Alamy Stock Photo; **p55**: Rob Walls/Alamy Stock Photo; **p56(m)**: ABC Collection/Alamy Stock Photo; **p56(b)**: John Mitchell/Science Source/Getty Images; **57(b)**: georgeclerk/iStockphoto; ***Extinct Giants cover***: Butterfly Hunter/Shutterstock; ***Safe in a Storm cover***: JanJar/iStockphoto; Umberto Shtanzman/Shutterstock; ***What Do We Need to Survive? cover***: Design Pics Inc/Alamy Stock Photo. All other photos by Shutterstock.

Contents Page

Tick the books you have finished.

The Portrait Problem

1   Look at page 2.
    Draw lines to show where the eyes, ears, nose and mouth
    should go.

eyes   ears

nose   mouth

2   What did Nadim think of Chip's portrait of Anneena?
    Tick the correct answer.

    ☐   He thought it wasn't much good.

    ☐   He thought it was brilliant.

    ☐   He thought the ears were not quite right.

    ☐   He thought it didn't look like her.

3   Why did Nadim want to keep Chip's portrait of him?
    Write the missing word to complete the sentence.

    Nadim thought that if Chip became a _____ artist,

    then the picture would be worth lots of money.

    famous   **tall**   **funny**

4   Look at Mrs May's instructions on page 2.
Colour the **two** portraits that followed Mrs May's instructions.

Jack

Anna

Anneena

Farisha

5   Why did Sandro's jars and pots fall on to the floor?
Tick the correct answer.

☐ There was an earthquake.

☐ Sandro threw them there in anger.

☐ The workmen knocked them over.

☐ The house was shaking.

6   Look at page 24. **"Place it on the very edge."**
What is *it* in this sentence?
Circle the correct answer.

the roof   **the frame**   **the painting**   **the boulder**

7 Look at page 26. **"The stone is unsafe. Remove it!"**
Why does the author use an exclamation mark?
Tick the **two** correct answers.

◻ to show that the weaver is whispering

◻ to show that the weaver is upset

◻ to show that the weaver is shouting

◻ to show that the weaver is happy

8 Which verbs show that someone is speaking in an unhappy way?
Circle the **two** correct answers.

laughed

wailed

smiled

groaned

9   Draw lines to match the words with their meanings.

bravo   equipment for making cloth

tunic   well done

loom   a long shirt

10   Write the missing words to complete the sentences.

does building jobs

paints pictures

makes cloth

An artist _____.

A weaver _____.

A workman _____.

11 How much did you enjoy the story and activities?
    Tick one picture to show how you feel.

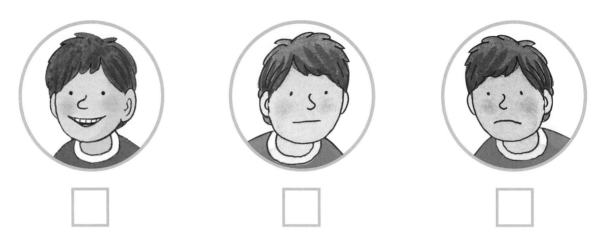

12 Draw a portrait of yourself or someone you know.
    Add a background.
    Look at page 1 of the story for some ideas.
    Write a sentence about the person.

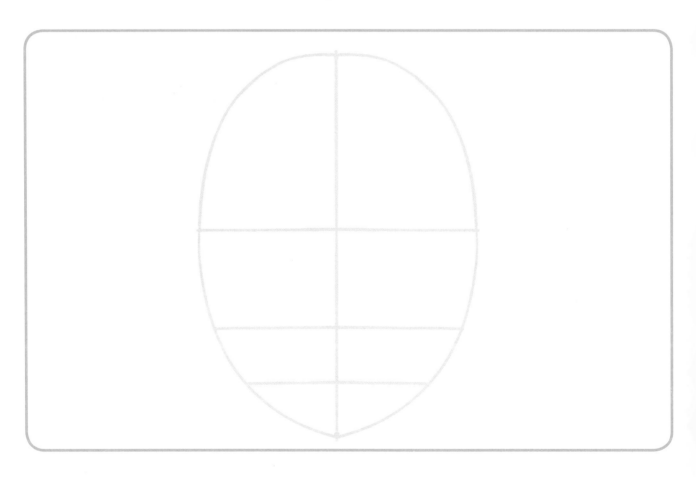

_____

_____

Book word count: 965

Detective Adventure

1   Look at page 3.
    What job does a detective do?
    Tick the correct answer.

    ☐   cleans up

    ☐   solves crimes

    ☐   writes books

    ☐   sells costumes

2   Write the missing word to complete the sentence.

    Anneena had the adventure on her own because Biff was busy

    taking the _____ down to Mum.

    dog   **tea**   **washing**

3   Look at page 12. **"The Duchess of Almond is here. She *was* wearing her diamond necklace."**
    Why is the word ***was*** in italics (slanting letters)?
    Tick the **two** correct answers.

    ☐   to show how the Inspector says this word

    ☐   to show that the Inspector is angry

    ☐   to show that the Inspector is whispering

    ☐   to show that the Duchess is not wearing the necklace now

4 Holmes says the necklace is **worth millions**.
   What does he mean?
   Tick the correct answer.

   ☐ It costs a lot of money.

   ☐ It is for sale.

   ☐ It belongs to a lot of people.

   ☐ It is very heavy.

5 Look at page 14. **"Two of my men were at the door all evening."**
   Who are *my men* in this sentence?
   Circle the correct answer.

   the butlers   **the thieves**

   the guests   **the police officers**

6 Which word has a similar meaning to **mystery?**
   Circle the correct answer.

   fog   **puzzle**

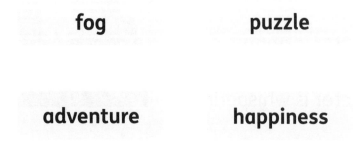

   adventure   **happiness**

7 Write the missing word to complete the sentence.

Anneena thinks it is odd to find a _____ in the bin.

glass   **ball**   **necklace**

8 Look at page 23. **"Stop!"**
Why does the author use an exclamation mark?
Tick the **two** correct answers.

☐ to show that Anneena is speaking loudly

☐ to show that Anneena is asking a question

☐ to show that Anneena is thinking

☐ to show that Anneena is excited

9   Look at page 30.
    Did the maid turn off the lights?
    Write yes or no.

    _____

10 In what order did these things happen?
    Write numbers 1 to 4 to show the correct order.

    ☐   The maid put the necklace inside the
        ball and threw it into the next room.

    ☐   The maid dropped a glass on purpose
        and picked up the ball as she cleared up.

    ☐   The butler switched off the lights and the
        maid stole the necklace.

    ☐   The maid hid the necklace in her pocket.

11   How much did you enjoy the story and activities?
      Tick one picture to show how you feel.

☐   ☐   ☐

12   Design a costume, for a book character, that you would like to
      wear in Book Week.
      Write a sentence saying who it is.
      Look at pages 1, 2 and 3 of the story for some ideas.

_____

_____

1 "A company in Tokyo wants to use the machine that Dad's company has invented. Dad has to show it to them."

What does *it* refer to?

Circle the correct answer.

Dad's company

the machine

the company in Japan

Tokyo

2 Write the missing word to complete the sentence.

The long flight made Mum feel very _____.

tired   excited   relaxed

3 "Welcome to Japan," said Rio shyly.

Underline the word which describes how Rio felt as she spoke.

4 Look at page 11.
Why would they never get Kipper out of the toy store?
Tick the correct answer.

☐ He would not be allowed to leave.

☐ He would be able to live there.

☐ He would have to pay to leave.

☐ He would not want to leave as there is so much to see.

5 **"Who are the men in robes?" asked Kipper.**
Why has the author used a question mark?
Circle the **two** correct answers.

Kipper wants to find out who the men are.

Kipper is excited to see the men.

Kipper knows who the men are.

Kipper is asking a question about the men.

6 Look at pages 22 and 26.
How do the pictures show that these events are on different days?
Tick the **two** correct answers.

☐ Biff has different clothes.

☐ There is a calendar.

☐ The weather is different.

☐ They are set in different countries.

7 **The mountain was capped with snow.**
Which word is closest in meaning to *capped*?
Circle the correct answer.

hidden   crushed   gleaming   topped

8 Draw lines to match the places with the correct pictures.

Mount Fuji

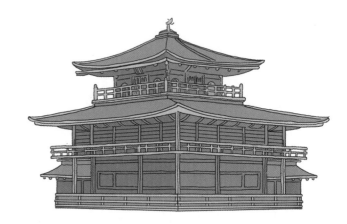

Golden Pavilion

temple in Tokyo

9   In what order did these things happen?
     Write numbers 1 to 4 to show the correct order.

     ☐   Mr Yamada took the family to their hotel.

     ☐   The children spoke to Rio online.

     ☐   The family flew to Japan.

     ☐   Yoko and Rio took the family sightseeing.

10   Draw lines to match the words with their meanings.

     arigato   Japanese robe

     chopsticks   Japanese word for 'thank you'

     kimono   sticks used to pick up food

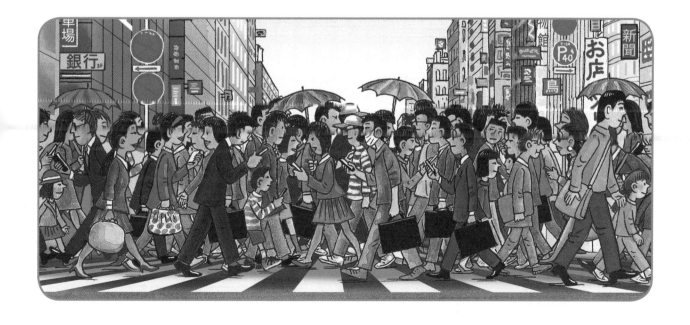

11 How much did you enjoy the story and activities?
    Tick one picture to show how you feel.

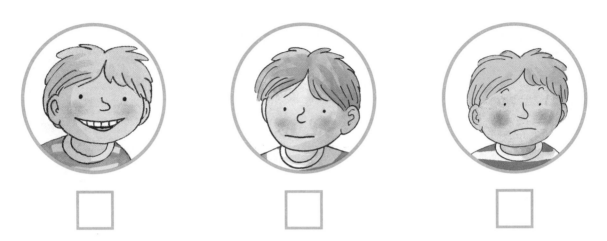

12 Design a postcard showing a place you have visited.
    Then write a message about it on the back of the card.

Front

Back

Book word count: 955

Magic Tricks

1   Look at page 2.
    Why does Wilf close his eyes and put his fingers on his forehead?
    Tick the correct answer.

    ☐   He has a headache.

    ☐   He is fed up of playing cards.

    ☐   He needs to sleep.

    ☐   He is pretending to think.

2   **The magic took them to the entrance of a fancy old theatre.**

    Which words describe what the theatre looks like?
    Underline the **two** correct words.

3   Write the missing words to complete the sentence below.

    On page 7 the author shows a picture of Marvo hiding and

    listening so that we understand how Marvo heard about

    the _____.

    magic trick   **magic key**

    theatre tickets

4 Look at page 11.
   What does the expression **put your hands together** mean?
   Circle the correct answer.

sit still	**wave**
clap	**hold someone's hand**

5 Draw lines to match the words with their meanings.

   dim   helper

   bow   bend over

   volunteer   not very bright

6 Which things came out of Marvo's hat?
   Tick the **two** correct answers.

   ☐ a rabbit

   ☐ a bird

   ☐ a key

   ☐ a glass of water

7 Write the missing words to complete the sentence.

Chip thinks Marvo stole the key when Biff was _____

_____.

on stage

in the entrance

in the dressing room

8 Look at page 27.
Why does Marvo have a confident grin?
Tick the correct answer.

☐ He thinks Wilf's trick won't fool him.

☐ He enjoys seeing new tricks.

☐ He is trying to be friendly.

☐ His theatre show went well.

9 Why couldn't Marvo understand how Wilf had done the trick?
   Tick the correct answer.

   ☐ because all the cards were the same

   ☐ because all the cards were different

   ☐ because all the cards were on the floor

   ☐ because all the cards were the nine of clubs

10 Write the missing words to complete the sentence.

   The story starts and finishes in _____

   _____ .

the theatre entrance

the bedroom at home

the theatre dressing room

11   How much did you enjoy the story and activities?
     Tick one picture to show how you feel.

☐   ☐   ☐

12   Draw something magical coming out of Marvo's hat.
     Write a sentence about it.

_____

_____

The Time Capsule

1   Look at page 1.
    What does Biff want to see?
    Circle the correct answer.

the school   the digger

the classroom   the swimming pool

2   Draw lines to match the words to their meanings.

loot   container

treasure   precious and valuable things

capsule   things that have been stolen

3   Look at page 16.
    What do the thought bubbles show?
    Tick the correct answer.

☐   ideas for a film

☐   how Chip imagines the future

☐   parts of a dream

☐   Chip's memories of the past

4 **Chip turned off the camera and sighed.**

Which word lets us know how Chip feels?
Underline the correct word.

5 Look at page 20. **Chip took the camera inside.**
Where inside does Chip take the camera?
Tick the correct answer.

☐ inside the school ☐ inside the capsule

☐ inside the swimming pool ☐ inside the house

6 Draw lines to match the things with how they go wrong.

ball

has a puncture

bike

gets burnt

dinner

gets stuck in the tree

7　How does Chip feel at each part of the story?
　Draw lines to match the events with
　Chip's feelings.

**seeing the builders
find the box**

disappointed

**when Mum gives
him a camera**

curious

**watching the film
he has made**

happy

8　What things do the family put in their time capsule?
　Tick the **three** correct answers.

☐ a shell

☐ a photo

☐ a football

☐ a film

9   In what order did these thing happen?
     Write numbers 1 to 4 to show the correct order.

☐

☐

☐

☐

10   Which words are things used by builders?
     Circle the **two** correct answers.

spade   box

digger   scrapbook

11   How much did you enjoy the story and activities?
     Tick one picture to show how you feel.

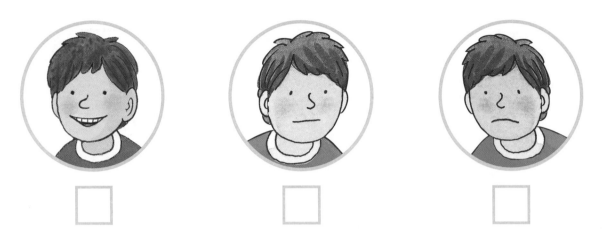

☐   ☐   ☐

12   Draw the things you would put in a time capsule.
     Add labels to your picture.

1 Look at page 2.
   Write the missing word(s) to complete the sentence.

   Uncle Max tells Biff, Chip and Kipper about his

   _____ adventures.

   night-time   **oldest**   **most recent**

2 Look at page 5.
   In Uncle Max's story, why do the jellyfish swim away?
   Tick the correct answer.

   [ ] They think Uncle Max wants to eat them with a spoon.

   [ ] They can see a shark coming.

   [ ] They don't like loud noises.

   [ ] They need to find food.

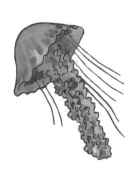
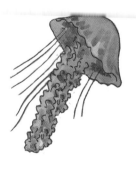

3   Look at page 8.
Write the correct word to complete the sentence.

drawing   **describing**

reading   **shouting**

The thought bubble shows what Uncle Max is _____.

4   **"You'd be surprised what can happen at sea," Uncle Max said.
"Once I ..."**
Why does the author use ... at the end?
Tick the correct answer.

☐   to show Uncle Max is lying

☐   to show Uncle Max has fallen asleep

☐   to show Uncle Max suddenly stops speaking

☐   to show the children are listening

5   **They stopped in a big, gloomy place.**
Which word is closest in meaning to *gloomy*?
Circle the correct answer.

sad   **dark**

damp   **empty**

6   In what order did these things happen?
    Write numbers 1 to 4 to show the correct order.

    ☐   Uncle Max and the children go on an adventure.

    ☐   A whale swallows Uncle Max and the children.

    ☐   Uncle Max gives some shells to the children.

    ☐   The magic key sends everyone home.

7   Which words describe how things sound?
    Which words describe how things look?
    Write the words under the correct headings.

    enormous   **gurgling**

    rumbling   **bright**

How things sound

_____   _____

_____

How things look

_____

_____

8   What does Uncle Max find on his sleeve?
    Colour the correct picture.

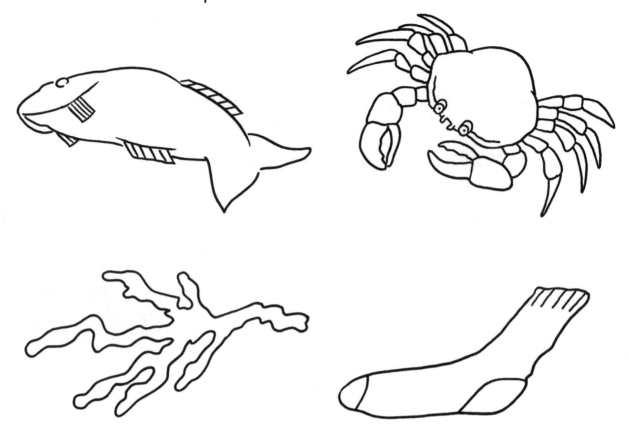

9   What do all Uncle Max's stories have in common?
    Tick the correct answer.

    [ ]   They are all about Biff, Chip and Kipper.

    [ ]   They are all about times when Uncle Max got hurt.

    [ ]   They are all set on a boat.

    [ ]   They are all set under water.

10 Are Uncle Max's stories true?
    Write yes or no.

    _____

11 How much did you enjoy the story and activities?
    Tick one picture to show how you feel.

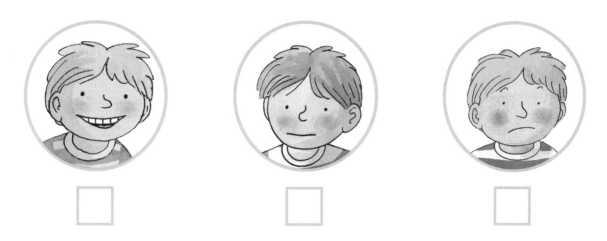

12 Draw yourself having an adventure at sea.
    Write a sentence about it.

1 Look at page 7.
   Write the correct word to complete the sentence.

   noisy   **hot**   **cold**

   Because the Earth was too _____ many animals became extinct.

2 **The megalodon (say meg-a-loa-don) lived millions of years ago.**
   What does the text inside the brackets tell us?
   Circle the correct answer.

   how to spell   what the dinosaur's
   the word   name means

   how to say   where to find more
   the word   information

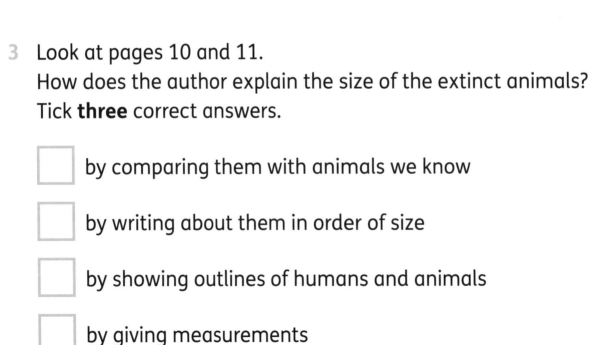

3 Look at pages 10 and 11.
   How does the author explain the size of the extinct animals?
   Tick **three** correct answers.

   ☐ by comparing them with animals we know

   ☐ by writing about them in order of size

   ☐ by showing outlines of humans and animals

   ☐ by giving measurements

4   Why did dodos become extinct?
    Tick **three** correct answers.

    ☐   Animals ate all of their eggs.

    ☐   An asteroid destroyed their habitat.

    ☐   Animals and people hunted them.

    ☐   They were easy to kill because they couldn't fly away.

5   Write the missing word to complete the sentence below.

    Steller's sea cows might have found it difficult to eat meat

    because they had no _____.

    teeth   **claws**

    stomachs

6   Draw lines to match the animals with the facts.

    elephant birds   **ate seaweed**

    Steller's sea cows   **the largest shark ever**

    megalodon   **lived on Madagascar**

7　This book is called *Extinct Giants*.
Which of the titles below would also make a good title for
the book?
Tick the correct answer.

☐　　　☐　　　☐　　　☐

8　Which sentences show facts?
Which sentences show opinions?
Write the word **fact** or **opinion** below each sentence.

Dodos are birds that are extinct now.

_____

Some scientists think that clouds of ash blocked out the sunlight.

_____

Elephant birds were over three metres tall.

_____

9 Which word is closest in meaning to **pouch**?
Circle the correct answer.

push   **pull a face**

hit   **pocket**

10 What are these animals called?
Draw lines to match the words to the pictures.

pelican

nautilus

horseshoe crab

11 How much did you enjoy the book and activities?
Tick one picture to show how you feel.

12 Draw the animal you like best in the book.
Write a sentence saying what you like about it.

_____

_____

Book word count: 826

A Mammoth Task

1 **"I'm feeling quite chilly in this wind," said Mum. "Come on! Let's go and get a hot drink."**
How does Mum feel?
Circle the **two** correct answers.

thirsty   **tired**   **cold**   **upset**

2 Which words show the effects of the storm?
Circle the **two** correct answers.

seaweed everywhere

sun was out

cliff had fallen down

people in the shops

3 Look at page 8. **"I think it *is* a bone," said Mum.**
Why is the word *is* in italics (slanted letters)?
Tick the correct answer.

☐ to show Mum is cross

☐ to make it look like a question

☐ to show how Mum says the word 'is'

☐ to make the page look more interesting

4   Write the missing words to complete the sentence.

Dad rings up to tell _____ about

the bone in the cliff.

Mrs May

his workmates

some experts

5   Does the bone come from a woolly mammoth?
    Write yes or no.

    _____

6   **"It's a pity the experts can't put the skeleton back together,"
    he said.**

    Which words tell us that Dad is disappointed?
    Underline the correct words.

7 What might happen if the experts put the mammoth's skeleton back together?
Tick the correct answer.

☐ the bones would not fit together

☐ the mammoth might come alive

☐ the skeleton would be too big

☐ the bones might break

8 In what order do these things happen?
Write numbers 1 to 4 to show the correct order.

☐ Dad builds a model mammoth.

☐ Wilma notices a bone.

☐ The experts excavate a steppe mammoth.

☐ The cliff collapses.

9 Write the missing word to complete the sentence.

People at a timber yard work with _____ .

metal   wood   stone   animals

10 Which word is closest in meaning to **task**?
Circle the correct answer.

horn   job   problem   bone

11 How much did you enjoy the story and activities?
    Tick one picture to show how you feel.

☐   ☐   ☐

12 Draw something you would like to build a model of.
    Add labels to your picture.

Safe in a Storm

1 Look at the Contents list.
  Where can you read about blizzards?
  Circle the correct answer.

page 16   **page 20**   **page 24**   **page 30**

2 Write the missing words to complete the sentence.

  A glossary in an information book is usually found _____

  _____.

  on the front cover   **at the end**

  at the beginning   **next to each heading**

3 Look at the picture of houses
  on page 4.
  Why do they look like that?
  Tick the correct answer.

☐ They are low down to shelter from the wind.

☐ They are high up because the ground floods.

☐ They have thick walls to give protection from the snow.

4 Write the missing word(s) to complete the sentence.

Heavy rain or snow that melts quickly can cause

sudden _____.

blizzards   **hailstorms**

flash floods

5 **From above, a hurricane looks like a swirling, giant cloud.**
Underline the word that tells us how the hurricane moves.

6 Look at page 17.
What has the author used to help us understand what a hurricane looks like?
Tick the **two** correct answers.

☐ a photo of an eye

☐ a photo of a hurricane

☐ an illustration of a hurricane

☐ a label pointing to the 'eye' of a hurricane

7   Why might windows break in a hurricane?
    Tick the **two** correct answers.

☐   They could shrink.

☐   The strong wind could break them.

☐   They could expand in the rain.

☐   Things being blown around could
     smash them.

8   Which things are dangerous?
    Which things are used for safety?
    Write the correct answers under the headings.

blizzards   shutters

lightning rod   flash floods

Danger

_____

_____

Safety

_____

_____

9   Which words are closest in meaning to **head indoors**?
    Circle the correct answer.

go inside   **block out the noise**

put your head inside   **go upstairs**

10 Look at page 28. **Hailstones are usually smaller than peas ...**
    What do the three dots mean?
    Tick the correct answer.

☐ They show the size of the hailstones.

☐ They show that someone is speaking.

☐ They show a pause in the sentence.

☐ They are a mistake.

11 How much did you enjoy the book and activities?
    Tick one picture to show how you feel.

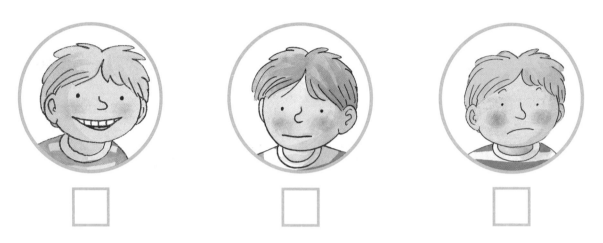

☐   ☐   ☐

12 Draw a scene with extreme weather.
    Write a sentence about what it would be like if you were there.

Book word count: 825

The Lightning Key

1   Look at page 5.
    What grew darker as the storm got closer?
    Circle the correct answer.

    the magic key   **the room**

    the lightning   **the stairs**

2   Look at page 10.
    Which word is closest in meaning to **experiment**?
    Draw a line from the word to the correct answer.

                                          test

    experiment   **company**

                                          question

3   Look at page 13. **"We need to find him!"**
    Why do you think the author uses an exclamation mark?
    Tick the correct answer.

    ☐   to show Biff is whispering

    ☐   to show Biff is worried

    ☐   to show Biff is happy

    ☐   to show Biff is puzzled

4 Why does the shopkeeper tell the children to get inside
   Will's house quickly?
   Tick the correct answer.

   ☐ because the sun is too hot

   ☐ so he can get home quickly

   ☐ they are not allowed to play outside

   ☐ so they don't get caught in the storm

5 Write the missing word to complete the sentence.

   Will's father is trying to _____ electricity.

   understand   **sell**   **make**

6 In what order do these things happen?
   Write numbers 1 to 4 in the boxes to
   show the correct order.

   ☐ Will drops his stuff.

   ☐ The children warn Will's father about the danger.

   ☐ The shopkeeper takes the children to Will's house.

   ☐ Will's father is flying a kite.

7 Draw lines to match the words with their meanings.

crackle   a short, sharp noise

rumble   screaming

howling   a deep banging noise

8 Why does the key look black and burned?
Tick the correct answer.

☐ It has been on a bonfire.

☐ It is broken.

☐ It has been left in the rain.

☐ The lightning has burned it.

9 **"No, that was our key," said Kipper, with tears in his eyes.**

Which words show how Kipper is feeling?
Underline the correct words.

10 Write the correct word to complete the sentence.

angry   **sad**   **relieved**

When Will shows the children he has the magic key,

they feel _____.

11 How much did you enjoy the story and activities?
Tick one picture to show how you feel.

☐ ☐ ☐

12 Draw a storm.
Write a sentence saying what is happening.

What Do We Need to Survive?

1   Write the correct word to complete the sentence.

faint   **die**

sweat

If humans don't drink water for a

few days, they will _____.

2   **Others use dams, wells, pipes and pumps to collect water ...**
What has the author used to separate the things in this sentence?
Circle the correct answer.

capital letters   **full stops**

commas   **speech marks**

3 Look at page 15.
What do the photos inside the circles show?
Tick the correct answer.

☐ the roots of the plant in the main photo

☐ close-up views of the underside of the big leaf

☐ close-up views of a different plant

☐ different plants from around the world

4 Do we use up more oxygen when we run
and jump than when we are sitting still?

Answer yes or no.

_____

5 Why don't animals that live on the deep sea floor eat plants?
Tick the correct answer.

☐ Deep sea plants are poisonous.

☐ It is too dark for them to find the plants.

☐ They don't need any food.

☐ It is too dark for plants to grow so there aren't any there.

6   Look at the food chain on page 22.
    What helps us to read the sentences in the correct order?
    Circle the correct answer.

the pictures   **the labels**

the arrows   **the words**

7   Draw lines to match the animals in the pictures with their names.

trout

vole

hawk

8 **You are part of a food chain too!**

What has the author used to show that this fact is a surprise?
Tick the correct answer.

☐ a full stop

☐ an exclamation mark

☐ the word 'you'

☐ the capital letter at the start

9 Look at page 26. Which words are closest in meaning to **repair**?
Tick the **two** correct answers.

☐ live

☐ fix

☐ break

☐ mend

10 Look at page 27. What foods do humans get from chickens?
Circle the **two** correct answers.

meat   **corn**

fish   **eggs**

11 How much did you enjoy the book and activities?
    Tick one picture to show how you feel.

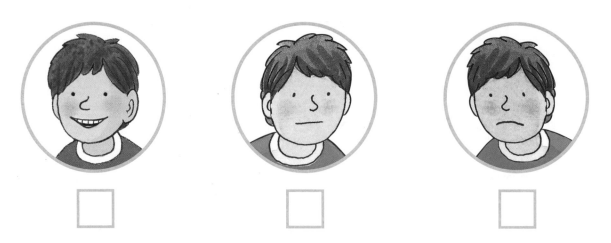

12 Draw an animal from the book and the food it likes to eat.
    Add labels to your picture.

Survival in the Arctic

1   **"Er ... you mean we're going to have to spend the night out here?"
    gasped Biff.**
    What does the word **gasped** tell you about how Biff is feeling?
    Tick the correct answer.

    ☐ She is shocked.   ☐ She is unsure.

    ☐ She is pleased.   ☐ She is angry.

2   What things help the children to survive a night in the snow?
    Colour in the **three** correct pictures.

3   Which words are vehicles?
    Tick the **two** correct answers.

    ☐ sled   ☐ fir

    ☐ snowmobile   ☐ eggs

4 What makes the noise that wakes Biff in the night?
   Circle the correct answer.

a helicopter   **a moose**

a bear   **a mouse**

5 **"The moose did us a good turn," he said.**
   What does ***did us a good turn*** mean?
   Tick the correct answer.

   ☐ helped us

   ☐ turned towards us

   ☐ did a good trick

   ☐ found us

6 What is the green pattern in the sky called?
   Circle the correct answer.

   the Coloured Curtain

   the Arctic

   the Northern Lights

   the Shower of Sparks

7 In what order did these things happen?
Write numbers 1 to 4 by the correct pictures.

8 What is the main idea in this story?
Tick the correct answer.

☐ Biff and Chip have to stay out all night in the Arctic.

☐ Dad, Biff and Chip have an adventure in the snow.

☐ Biff and Chip see a moose.

☐ Biff and Chip decide that they don't really like the snow.

9   Draw lines to match the words with their meanings.

stump   staying alive

settled down   a bit of tree trunk

survival   got comfortable

10   Why does Kitchi get the fire to make smoke?
     Tick the correct answer.

☐ to scare off wild animals

☐ to cook the fish

☐ he enjoys making smoke patterns

☐ to signal to the rescue team

11 How much did you enjoy the story and activities?
Tick one picture to show how you feel.

☐   ☐   ☐

12 Draw a snow activity you would enjoy.
Write a sentence explaining what it is.

_____

_____

My Words

Write your favourite new
word from each book.

_____

_____

_____

_____

_____

_____

_____

_____

_____

_____

My Badges

Stick your badges here.